supermodernprayerbook

SUSAN BRADLEY SMITH began her writing life as a music and theatre journalist in Sydney and later London. Since then she has published extensively as a theatre and literary historian. Her first collection of poems, *Marmalade Exile*, was described as 'Plath unleashed'. She lives at the beach with her husband and three of their children, and teaches in the English Department at La Trobe University, Melbourne.

Also by Susan Bradley Smith

POETRY
    Marmalade Exile (Southern Cross University Press, 2006)

PLAYS
    Griefbox (Salt Publishing, 2001)

supermodernprayerbook

SUSAN BRADLEY SMITH

SALT
LONDON

PUBLISHED BY SALT PUBLISHING
Dutch House, 307–308 High Holborn, London WC1V 7LL United Kingdom

© Susan Bradley Smith, 2010

The right of Susan Bradley Smith to be identified as the
author of this work has been asserted by her in accordance
with Section 77 of the Copyright, Designs and Patents Act 1988.

Salt Publishing 2010

Printed in Great Britain by the MPG Books Group, Bodmin and King's Lynn

Typeset in Swift 9.5 / 13

ISBN 978 1 84471 449 0 paperback

1 3 5 7 9 8 6 4 2

for Ulrike Bliss

Contents

Acknowledgements

Some of these poems have been previously published in *Over There: Poems from Singapore and Australia* and *Verse*. I would like to thank James (especially), Tim (for the musical collaboration), the poetry students at La Trobe University, and my friends, family and colleagues.

invocation

to remind ourselves that god is everywhere, to remind ourselves
to invite god in, to remind ourselves that it is already too late
to do otherwise because god got to us before we got to god,
to remind ourselves that yes god is closer to us than our own
breath, our own feet, so come on in . . .

Sea monsters

You will never have to loan
her money, or pretend you
like her husband, or agree
with her parenting skills, or
even advise about university
or work let alone what tampons
are worth trying and which
GP has the nicer touch for
pap smears. All these things
that you worried about, and
a million others, what a waste
that anguish was. Perhaps instead
you should have followed your
gut instinct, that bile which doesn't
lie, and never have let her go to the
party, where she drank iced-lolly
drinks from thin-necked bottles,
and took a small sophisticated
tablet from a boy, who had two
others standing behind him,
slyly enjoying the strain of
their cocks in their jeans. They
went to the beach—you should
have warned her about that too,
beach parties—and forced
themselves into all of her
three holes, for fun, it was
such a laugh.

And now you sit there, saved forever from her needs, and your responsibilities, because she sorted herself out, swam out past the breakers after they had left her to recollect herself, maybe it was a shark or maybe she swam to Atlantis, either way you will never see her again. Her best friend saw it all, and those boys caught her, played their golf, again. *Shut up bitch* they said but she never did. Until now. She sits besides you, the utter disbelief at the judge's decision *Fine young men undone by drink and circumstance* making your womb ache and her eyes twitch. You both hold white roses. Someone behind you says *thank god* and sobs, grateful for their son's salvation. Your hands are bleeding. Community service. The pain is insuperable. You know now that you will kill.

Country towns are such a hoot.

I could not do this ever again

It is done.
I am hiding in the car, cradling memory,
crying, my cheek, squeaking against the
window, sodden.

Cradling memory,
I am hiding in the car, in the garage, still
bloody, my own arms gladwrapping me,
cauterizing the tears.

Still now. Bloody
still. I hang on. I don't let go. I hang on.
hunting for a tissue, some makeup, I find
instead your photo.

Hang on. You are
five years old, in black and white, grinning
at me like Christmas, the tinsel image of your
happiness brands me.

We belong. I hang on.
We belong. I leave the garage, enter the house,
walk outside, find sex-kitten, thirteen-year-old
you beside the pool.

You are thirteen. You
loll by the pool like a Hollywood starlet, eating
popcorn, your feet in the water, your heart in the
stars, your mess in my kitchen.

You brand me.
You are thirteen. Your mess is in my kitchen
and soon I will cook your supper and recall
that you once loved me.

Trouble is pastel
and smells like yesterday and once, you loved
that I was your mother. Blood is black, and I
have just killed your kin.

Once. I sigh my
abortionist's sigh, you smile, and plead over your
sunblessed shoulder for your favourite food.
I answer. Yes. I love you. I answer.

9481 5046

She was lonely that's why she'd started doing it, speed-
    dialling strangers on the inherited
phone, found, full of numbers, abandoned, in her new
    Melbourne apartment, where

she was a stranger in a world-class city, a Sydney kind of
    stranger, always lusting for the
ocean and its pacific tug of freckled hope, lost now, like her
    child

and her husband, because once they'd seen her in the
    morgue, they could never recover
their touch for each other, even their last kiss goodbye felt
    like rape, felt like

the mistake of a dream where you accidentally slept with
    your father, and this made them
suddenly unmarried and ashamed that they'd ever even so
    much as held hands, and for

her, in a new apartment where everything came from IKEA
    and there was little hope of
staining anything, that is why talking to someone else's
    pre-packaged life smelt like

Love.

All day long, walking around in a Tennessee Williams play

At first I wasted time looking around for the film crew, surely such hi-jinx needed this erudition, but no, there they were, three big men, not even students, they were middle-aged and had the girth of people who lived and indulged, they were laughing, as they launched their rockets on the university lawn, outside the Humanities block, near the moat, amongst the duckshit and the lunching youth — one such actor had just returned my dropped purse, with a strange kindness, then walked off shyly to class.

> Rockets.
> Made of recycled plastic bottles.
> *Watch your heads*
> They said
> Upon descent.

One of them had a model helicopter. Were they scientists? Was this like Sunday tennis for men of this faculty? Why did they like each other when they didn't have to? And how do adults make friends, anyway, without children as barter? In the English Department we don't do lunch, except *al desko*. We're too busy to even manage a Christmas function. Although I have heard it rumoured there's drinks on Thursday nights, for those whose children have graduated from need.

And yet here they are, those men, unconcerned by corridors and their politics, eating sandwiches and making small banging miracles.

> Galahs.
> The galahs from their castle gums
> Screamed

Fuck off you idiots this is a university
And flew off, disgusted.

They started to pack up. No one wanted them to finish their games. The sky was as blue as a day-spa infinity pool. They might as well have owned the whole campus, all forty years of its mighty crunch. Their small red car waited for them, like a cherry bomb, on the gravel road. How would they all fit in? Where would they go, now that the boot had echoed its snap, and it was all over? If they'd pulled out a pipe, I would have followed. The bell tower began its midday raucous, mad, mad lumps of falling brass chasing each other, crying out to the soft skies of Bundoora, a thousand miles from Melbourne's care.

Bells.
I love you I love you I love you
This is the sound of Europe
Calling. I can never hear them
From my office.

Molecules, plural: a daughter is born

The telephone rang, and made that
glottal burp, signifying Germany, and
there it was, your voice, bass and built
for opera. You would not sign the papers

without asking me, one more time. Would
I, reconsider? Another chance to let you
unlove me, another chance to let your
mother hate me, another damn chance. I

left because I do not understand aftershave, I
do not understand how death will decide
me, I do not understand my relationship
to commerce. But I do know this, soldier:

Once, you kissed me, and it will never stop.

Our own allotted toil

It has come to pass:
we live our lives like giants
walking into the
cinema, the film over,
heiss, howling for a rerun.

The idiocy of umbrellas

Mournful shadows layer the Strand. Last night he said,
he said to me that Alexander Pope and Lady Mary
(who's she when she's at home?) began a lifelong quarrel
shortly after an exchange of love letters. Lifelong. He did
not have the stamina for my perpetual disappointment,
he said, as though he were not to blame, and left. Off he
flew, like Mary Poppins' faggot, into the November
evening, already long and grey with beauty, the black trees
fingering their own sky. It was grey, cashmere grey, that sky.
All over London, the usual girls were kissing the usual men,
and I was left contemplating the protruding witchery of trees.
So the next morning, I was glad of the rain, and my umbrella,
pleased at its cheery cherry redness, and its ability to
curtail the contemplation of sky, and naked trees, whilst on
my way to work.

I saw their feet first, how odd, summer sandals, high
and silver for her, and he was wearing thongs. Flip flops.
Stupid, colourful, slappy shoes. He was walking slightly
ahead of her, downhill to Temple Station, the mist of rain
now like surreal confetti, for clearly, they were united. Her
hippy walk said of him, *He's been bonking me all night long, all
night,* her body honey, sinew, his. He turned, smiled, laughed.

I wanted some of that. I followed them into the intestines of that
Goddess of modernist transport, the underground, I went below
with them, already Saturn's disciple, stood beside them on the
platform. I could push them both, and be done with it, call it
a phone slap too far, email the picture of their butchered love to
the world before I was even arrested. But there we stood,
politely, being announced to, waiting, living, packing up pocket

umbrellas. She dropped a white cotton handkerchief at her feet. He knelt before her, and kissed one wet knee with solid intention. Then, the other. She trembled in her wizard's shoes. As he stood, he turned and caught my stare. I didn't care. He licked a drop of rain from his upper lip. He was wet and I was not. He leant into me, pushed his lips to my ear, *I just love this weather, don't you?*

Fucking hippies. It came in a tidal rush, the train, all wind and metal and duty. Like fish who must never stop moving for fear of demise, we joined the journeyers prepared, *another day another dollar for the botox nurse*, ready to do as we should, for we are all such sluts for capitalism. For capitalism, we spread our legs. The seats were those of bristled, multi-coloured corduroy, prickly, I imagine, if you were bare-legged. I am not. They have disappeared.

I wish the English would talk more, on the Tube.

The Scarlet series of true belief

The stress underwent its adrenalin transformation
when her lip suddenly curled as I offered my breast,
panic became me, and although we were two blocks
away, in A&E, within 10 minutes, her coma lasted
a thousand times longer than that, it had its own
smoke and smell and they linger still in my blood.

Jumpoline.
Footyball.
Eleventeen.
Baby Anabelle
did a smell

I've seen I've seen I've seen
her live and grow, post diagnosis,
but she remains forever grey in the
retina between me and reality. I pray,
and take too many photos, in case
the smoke finds a way to escape.
Please, draw me a person.

To step on a mother

Oh Bless me for I have sinned again. They were all
so crisply cheerful, as only the English in Edinburgh
can be, and she fed his stray baby daughter, at her own
wedding feast, it seemed bequeathed to her, this

task of black crows. She had no father or brother or
friends, they'd all RSVPd with regret, it perhaps
tasted like hers, of pork sausage and cold potato.
She was pregnant anyway and full of the last nonsense

of beauty, it slipped out of her, hers, with the
afterbirth, after all that. She was old enough to
know better — is there anything lonelier than
shopping by yourself for bridal shoes? There is

living your life with strangers, I suppose. There
is that. They both smell the same, like a woman
infected by the smell of another woman, transferred
by the same man. Fertile noonday trespass

that was meant to be a goodbye, a final return
to find the cricket kit and the lost record and you
end up having to pay for that last respect for the
next twenty five years. Beginning with feeding

said politeness at your own nuptials while your
groom dances with less expectant women. The
anniversary looms and she buys broad presents, it
is more fun than shopping all alone for wedding

shoes (has she mentioned this already?) the King's
Road slapping faces with its rich rain and abortionist
echoes. The world and its abortions, and its lonely
shoppers. They have a life size merry-go-round in Daisy

and Tom's. Her daughters, they will all have their very first
hair cuts there. She will witness the scissors and their swift
promises, but for now, tonight, she will dine
out with him, her fox, and the forgiving moon.

You are my charm pistol, my mother-in-law, my megalodon

Greatest ancestor of the great white shark, mother of my
husband, lost
You birthed him as trilobite, an ecological groovster, a
biker, a clown
Roaring away with a premature lust, like hagfish mucus,
laced with frost
But with those eyes you can navigate while swimming
upside down.

You birthed him as trilobite, an ecological groovster, a
biker, a clown
To learn only that we have evolved from sea squirts, bags of
jelly, our hearts
But with those eyes you can navigate while swimming
upside down
Why not the alien physiology of a giant squid, three hearts,
nine brains: such parts

To learn only that we have evolved from sea squirts, bags of
jelly, our hearts
God gave us such impressive eyes to better avoid each
other, mantra shrimps, all
Why not the alien physiology of a giant squid, three hearts,
nine brains: such parts
I miss the shoal of you, your high-tech predation, your odes
to extinction, your call.

God gave us such impressive eyes to better avoid each other,
　　mantra shrimps, all
To survive such onslaught, such predation—those genes
　　are worth passing on
I miss the shoal of you, your high-tech predation, your odes
　　to extinction, your call.
Water is eight hundred times denser than air, and squids
　　die after they breed: gone.

To survive such onslaught, such predation—those genes
　　are worth passing on
Roaring away with a premature lust like hagfish mucus,
　　laced with frost
Water is eight hundred times denser than air, and squids
　　die after they breed: gone.
Greatest ancestor of the great white shark, mother of my
　　husband, lost.

confession

to remind ourselves to transcend barriers of pain that inhibit forgiveness, to remind ourselves to seek the sunshine of full love, to remind ourselves that it is a folly to hide things from ourselves, from god, to remind ourselves that forgiveness follows the true sorrow of searching self-examination, to never forget the sadly truncated thing that is confession without amendment . . .

London traffic

On her beautiful, betraying hands
twist twist twisted, are her husband's rings, soapy still
from the rushed bath. Trophies,
she twirls them.

The traffic has stopped at the
Strand. They are late, the colleagues, for an important date,
she is sick and he sorry, beside her, in their
black taxi brothel.

Suddenly, speeding along Waterloo
Bridge in the rain, with an entangled nimbleness they manage
to hold hands. Sweet liberty sparks anew,
the hangovers, forgotten.

Apparently, he has three or four
women he kisses, she, on the other hand, has little understanding
of lips, loves her daughter with a foreign surprise
and needs no contraception.

The husband, the wife, the children
are certain to be remembered, honoured, but not now. They
kiss like history first discovering the ocean, till,
turning a final corner, the traffic dies.

Later, they will walk towards home,
back across the mighty Thames, completely insane with the late
summer night and *what is it about London anyway?* but
right now, on this road, they are stuck.

The whole world is falling
apart, where are the gods to deny? Yes, they will dance with
destiny's sweetest masturbations, but for now they sit without
touching, the two of them going nowhere.

Dogshit park and other suburban nightmares

This is a story about why Miranda gave up writing to work
    in Asda, where
the checkouts hum like women used to before they knew
    how to use vibrators,

and it goes like this, the making of that decision, which was
    based upon the following
facts: fictive parenting in contemporary Hackney is
    something that novelists

do rather well, it is virtual in accuracy, pitch, and reach—
    whereas poets write
poems like depressed naturalists, all brutal accuracy
    without brightness. You can

see their pain everywhere, these confessional giants with
    their abuse of visibility,
acting with the blithe belief that newborns will never learn
    to read. However,

novelists take so long to tell a story that you could visit
    every park in Greater
London before they were done with their unfaithful
    diplomacies. None of it is

heart surgery, Miranda resolves. Not all litter deserves to be
    recycled. In Asda,
you can buy anything. They laugh in the staffroom. In Asda
    you can buy lots of wine.

Awful

In seventy-three days
we'll be in Denmark
being smart together
at some conference
phoning spouses and
singing lullabies to
children. I hope to be
doing this blanched
from the epic grief of
you having first taken
me in your arms then
never forgetting me.

The thing about you is
this (stop looking at me
like that to start with) it
is, and I know this to be
true because I've never
read your books, it is not
destiny, it is not lust, it is
just the impossibility of
not ever touching you.

This morning you showed
me your new coat, uncertain
(she doesn't like it) I promised
(you laughed) to embrace you
each time in every corridor
of all the universities I saw you
wearing it. Cheek. (Is it time,
now, to tell you?) I touched the

cloth, you were so, so still, and
then I said *Maybe I like different*
things about you than she does.
'Maybe you do'.

The thing about me is this. When
my baby died last year I cut a hole
in my breast and willed it never
to heal. And when I came back
home from grief I was nobody's
wife. So if it is sad for you that our
affair would harm small worlds
then it is a tragedy for me to return
to love so badly.

The first time we kissed it was
your birthday, the gods had put our
small children between us to stop me
from spilling blood, for without them,
risk would be an ancient memory
and we would both now be well
slaughtered with love. It was your
decision to trespass me with your lips.
Thank you, you said, for the present.

We're on the radio, in the newspapers,
current affairs, doing our job and
changing the world yet I am paralysed,
unable to say the one thing I know:
that once upon a time in Surry Hills
I passed you in a crowded pub and

shuddered perhaps but saw no reason
to turn around nor suspect the long
black thread of surgery that unites me
forever putrid to you. And the band
played on, and the moon shone down,
last Friday night, my friend, in Bloomsbury.
It caught me, in love, on the footpath,
sharing a cigarette, your family's groceries
at our feet. And now, you're out to lunch,
with your wife. Somewhere in London.

Anger in a double string of pearls

I forgive you, she said,
harvesting another mouthful
of beetroot risotto.
He was having steak,
they always liked opposites,
it was fun once, but
now it only worked in
restaurants, and so the
years wore on. I'm
sorry, he said, his cutlery
sentries now, awaiting
reanimation. She made
good promise of her rocket
salad while his hand
trembled the red wine,
glassed high above the river.
That was Chicago, this is
Brisbane, she said. You
were away. You shouldn't
go away. He had remembered
her when young, he had come in
the sarcophagus of her. He
wanted her back. Can you
still love me, he asked of his meat.
The young waitress, with
her undergraduate ambitions,
did not believe a word of
any story, she'd heard them all,
had accounts for all of them.
Eat, said the woman. I hate waste.

gebrauchsfertig

Get yourself ready baby, for while I am pausing
at corners, of which I am overly fond, it has
agreeably remained with me, this idea
of being your mistress.
Oh yes.

You let
me dip my finger in
your wine, you tell me that all will
be well, but when London ceases to be
London, come August, I know the shape of swell.

The moon smells

like gunpowder. I heard tonight
that you were in trouble. I'm not
here to help, let me tell you.
I have a gun cocked at your
need, rock solid and covered in
denim. Spoil me, spill over
me. Me, I was size seven and now
I'm sorry you're so old that
you've had a heart attack.
My heart has long suffered thus,
the need for surgery.

Any better nature I might possess

Deserted me when I
Read your letter—
I know I would be
Happy, if only I could
Live with you. Again.
It jumped right up out
Of my throat and clung
To the new light fitting.
I wrote you a cheque
Instead of a letter and
Cut my tongue licking
The envelope. You were
Crazed and helpless, I'm
Sure, but Jesus did bid us
Shine in our own small
Corners. So I sat in mine,
And looked upwards to
The clear light, hoping for
The reprieve of grace,
But it had vanished,
That better nature of mine:
In this world is darkness.

Things I remember (I wanna marry Joey Ramone)

Marky liked cocktails and flirting with waitresses
and Joey liked lobster mornay (thermidor being
too sophisticated a word for the restaurant, for the deck,
for the sunshine, for Australia itself) and ordered bourbon
and they all drank on, sinking into the rolling rock of
the Sydney harbour sunset, their performance hours,
continents away. Give me give me give me the shock
of a man to love, a man who can sum up the world
in less than two epic hardcore minutes, and who can
remember your name all the way across the Atlantic,
even though you lost it yourself, there, last time you
saw him, on the carpet at a party in Brixton, or was it in
the plastic beer cups, á l'Academie, or was that someone
else's long lost life? Dead, dead, dead, and the pinheads
may rule again, but this morning my son rifled through
the strewn albums at his still two-year-old feet and jumped
on the choices for his Wednesday birthday party. 'No sleep
till Hammersmith' and 'Leave Home', and I thought of
the sharp-edged promise of oysters, before, during, and
after sex, and already I can feel love leaving me, off to kill
another girl *Oh I love her so*. Full stop.

I remember you.

She turned me on

You were off,
you insisted,
off. How could
you, then, fuck
her? Tell me that.
Why, how, I insist:
she turned me on.

I insist also on
you cataloguing
your sorrow to
litmus my own.
You shame your
biology, your gender:
she turned me on.

That's my job,
I thought, mistress
that I am. How is it
that you unemployed
your lust, your
promise, for me?:
she turned me on.

One day it will come to this: I'll be dying and years ago we'll
have divorced our paths only crossing at our children's
weddings and there was the funeral as well wasn't there and
you'll still have no idea of how or when I stopped loving you
because after all she was your wife goddamn it and I was
somebody else's wife in bed with my own husband and you were
on the living room floor was it or in your bedroom how did she

actually make you get it up was it superbly executed fellatio or
just her nakedness or did you fancy ... whatever I am with child
you whore you whoring scag my bones are unmarrowed with
forgiveness.

It is the rising sword
between us (history)
that will one day strike
me down for my hatred,
for your cowardice, but
most of all for your honesty:
she turned me on.

They say that men think about sex every six minutes you
    said it was quicker
than that, your betrayal. What a short sweet waste of my
    whole life.

Landeshauptstadt Stuttgart

I like the long words of you, 'widow
of the captain of the ship that sunk' —
English does not tongue every experience
there is to be had. You Germans, you
know there is purchase in acts of
gross concealment, you know that
such words give you entire
unimagined worlds to keep for
yourself. Just you, and those words.

You du you sie you du you sie you du du du.

What is 'gross' you ask, and is
anything bigger than Stuttgart?
That mother city of all Schwabenland,
I am ready to ask her some questions,
I am, about you. You and your fidelities,
someone must be to blame, some siren
whore sitting on a rock somewhere
with wet hair, making you turn your
back, forever, on Sydney's sweeter sins.

You du you sie you du you sie you du du du.

We have a daughter, you know, she likes to
spit her nazi venom at me sometimes, it is one of
life's lonelier acts, mopping up your children's
hatred, all alone. One day, she will stand atop the
hill of rubble made from the ruins of your bombed-
out birthplace, dreaming of a nobler Pforzheim, of

Roman towers and aqueducts, and maybe even
brownshirted youths, sunshine splitting their smiles:
sewage will be witnessed on this journey back to earth.

It was once only ever you. *Du du du.* When will this be through?

The guardian of things lost

Today she learnt about the amygdala,
the part of her brain that processes

emotions, and began to wonder about
the sure aim of lobotomists. Panic

became her, she knelt down among
the field of small fountains in Somerset

House and prayed for divorcees, for the
school yard, for the mass murderer, for

the mother who lost her daughter to a
bomb in a bus off Russell Square, prayers

for groupies, prayers for the bitch who's
going to get it for humiliating her in front

of her children. Somewhere, she thought,
standing, I have a credit card with purchase.

thanksgiving

to remind ourselves of the natural gratitude of the heart, to remind ourselves not to take things for granted, to remind ourselves not to forget the grace that is embodied in gift, and when all joy is woven into landscapes that form the backdrop to our lives, to recall what life would be like without the glue behind the wallpaper . . .

Anniversary

Separation, whether you want it or not,
intimacy, whether you want it or not, this
is what the night brings. We walk home
from our evening out, beneath the trees
posing as judges, the shifting sheets of
moonlight blessing us through the leaves.

You walk too fast, my heel breaks, I am
frightened of owls. We had drunk ourselves
to a clinking anger, but you kiss me at the
corner, making stiff amends. All over the
twinkling city, men say sorry and women
sigh. My god, you are good at everything.

You're twenty two weeks pregnant

I was frightened when I
saw your email. 'Things
are pretty good here', you
wrote, and then your
luminosity failed me,
tripped me up with its
breathtaking news, like
claws. You are pregnant. I
thought you did not love,
anymore, I thought that
he had secret women in
every state of the land, and
you, perhaps the grocery boy.
But no. No, you had the
same thing I suppose that
you'd always had, and have —
patience, and memories of
madder times, the best of
times, when your love
was the cloth of every
tepee in North America,
and you both slept within
that shelter. I went south,
long ago. You go well.

The poetess at Collingwood pool
for Dorothy Porter

This winter has been full of long-distance phone calls, you
telling me that petrol is one pound twenty a litre, outrageous,
England is, but please don't mistake these mundane exchanges
for presentism: you are long absent, and today I nearly
drowned our daughter, try putting that on a postcard. The

witness could not have been more impressive. Collingwood
pool was a steaming asylum, the high glass walls screaming
out to constipated rainbows, it was beautiful. First, fifty
minutes of serious rain, then the sunshine slutting around. The
roof was groaning as she emerged from the changerooms, the

famous Sydney poetess, looking herded by the school holiday
hordes invading her Tuesday. At first she did not recall me, had
never seen me in swimmers with wet hair, had not known about
my too many children, all mad screamers—why would she know
me like this, I barely did? Things were getting too dangerous to

talk, business men were lunch-time lapping and my slippery
six-year-old had floated with as much innocence as a box jellyfish
into the fast lane. A man-machine was about to harvest her with
his fisty fin, I went to save her but pulled her under instead of
lifting her over the plastic cork rope, dividing lanes. I am so

frightened of upsetting even strangers that it seems I would
first murder my young. In her seal eyes, afterwards, I could see
that this was not the first time I had betrayed her. I can never
alter this, this computation. I am so sorry, so so sorry, I say it
over and over again as the poetess watches. I say it again and

again, holding her, loving her more than when she was born. She softens. Sobbing turns to porridge turns to dandelion wishes. My lips suck her cheek, slowly, chlorine punishment, she lets me. I am forgiven, loved, beheld. The poetess sits on the pool's edge now, she waves. The children play, the lappers slap on, and we

talk softly of remembered promises to visit. Outside, the weather cracks, but in this wet ark all we are is the future. Next month, the mother of all Medusas will cancer the poetess away. The rain will stay. You, twelve thousand miles away with your other children, your first family, you can never, ever touch these unskilled weeks.

The last time
for Hunter

You smiled at me.
You were lying on
your right side, in
bed, across from me,
and I smiled back. I
was in love. I had been
feeding you every
two hours since you
were born, and now,
now it was over. Not
just for you, but for me,
forever. My last baby,
my only boy, my long
lost chance to mother
properly, now a grave
in Hackney, wet clay
claws that bury cuts of
my cubed heart, alongside
that smile. For come
tomorrow, you are the
nanny's, for ever and
ever amen, and I once
more become a lost
creature of the Tube,
taking my aching self
to drip all over the stairs
of the university. 'Read',
I will say, 'and recall
love's function', and
my students will smell
the robot lie of me as I

stand, a million floors of
tower high, with my back
to the London Eye, the
big wide sky raping me
through the box of window.

Cupid and Psyche renounce Ritalin, family therapy, and Facebook

The way you wake up, still asleep, velvet-skinned
The way you let your hair grow absently long
The way you showed me Ditchling and the Sussex Downs
The way you used to pump petrol and take care of your mum
The way you mourn your father though he is still alive
The way you were alone, from seven years old, at boarding school
The way you jangle beer bottle tops in your pockets
The way your legs are strong and long and meant for cricket
The way you decided to leave her, and your children, and come to me
The way your first girlfriend betrayed you and screwed your mate
The way your tattoos shimmer as you make love to me
The way your touch triggers synaesthesiatic life
The way your babies need your gentle converge
The way you drink too much, and forget to buy milk
The way you sneak, and snoop, into business that is not yours
The way you read to our children, smelling their heads
The way you pound your hands on walls, and hate
The way you kneel before me, swearing you are the one
The way that you stay. The way that you will go.

In forensic praise of you (a poem for two voices)

for emily xyz

between us	between us
between the sheets	between the sheets
between the good times and the bad	between the good times and the bad
between memory and loss	between memory and loss
between the lines	between the lines
between black and white	between black and white
between	between
between	between
between	between
between black and white	between black and white
between the lines	between the lines
between memory and loss	between memory and loss
between the good times and the bad	between the good times and the bad
between the sheets	between the sheets
between us	between us
you	it'll be alright
love	it'll be alright
me	it'll be alright
you	in the long run
love	in the long run
me	in the long run
not	it'll be alright
you	it'll be alright
love	it'll be alright
me	in the long run
you	in the long run
love	in the long run
me	it'll be alright

[46]

not   it'll be alright
you   it'll be alright
what?
what was that you said?   you
say it again   love
say it again   me
say it again   you
what was that you said?   love
say it again   me
say it again   not
say it again   you
what was that you said?   love
say it again   me
say it again   you
say it again   love
what was that you said?   me
what was that you said?   not

it'll be alright   supplication and entreaty
it'll be alright   supplication and entreaty
it'll be alright   you came
in the long run   once more
in the long run   to my bed
in the long run   (fuck me, fuck my head)
it'll be alright   and I gave you my body
it'll be alright   loving myself lonely
it'll be alright   dislocating my wife life
in the long run   I was not there
in the long run   I was not there
in the long run   passport please
it'll be alright

it'll be alright   please
it'll be alright

                                         passport please
                                         please

Barbie was
originally
a dildo
a Swiss dildo   a dildo
the cultural history of   a golden
Barbie was argued out   dildo
in the courts of America
all in order
to own   the courts of America
an image
a doll
the world, and all the
    money
in all the world   a doll
is nothing more than this—   all the money
a walk through   all
the tame gardens   the
of midnight Zurich   money
whilst dreaming gently   a doll
of golden insertion

                                         dreaming gently
golden insertion   of golden insertion

my wife life
dislocating my wife life

it'll be alright

[48]

between us

it'll be alright

between us

it'll be alright

between us

it'll be alright

between us

it'll be alright
in the long run   in the long run
in the long run   in the long run
in the long run   in the long run

you know   hum
we fuck   hum
every night   ho
but I still haven't   hum
done   ho
talking   ho
to you   hum
     talking
     to you

between the good times and
    the bad   between the good times and
        the bad
between the good times and
    the bad   between the good times and
        the bad
between the good times and
    the bad   between the good times and
        the bad

'she turned me on'
that's my job I thought
'she turned me on'

I insist on you	she
cataloguing your confession	turned
to litmus my sorrow	him
your biology shames you	on
you with your cock	was
and its endless needs	all
but how did you actually	she
unemploy your love for me?	did
I would rather the gentle	she
lie of rape than to	turned
believe that men think	him
about sex very six	on
minutes (do you?)	and
you said it was	on
quicker than that	and
your betrayal	on
what a short	and
sweet	on
waste	oh
of my	oh
whole	oh
life.	baby
She turned him on.	
Oh baby.	oh baby
Now I'm off.	
Off.	yeah
What about our babies?	
Is that all there is between us?	
Between us	Between us

[50]

Between us   Between us
Between us   Between us
Between us   Between us
Between us   Between us
between   between
between   between
between   between
us   us
us   us
us   us
I need to praise you.
Like I should.
Like I should.   like you should
                              stop being so forensic
baby   baby
yeah
I'll stop.

Stop   Stop

On the day that I died

When he first kissed me, that first real
kiss, not a stolen one, but one that can survive
marriage and one of you tasting of tea and
the other of coffee, that is what today also
shook slightly from — perfection. Oh perfect day,
how have I spent it with you? To begin with, we
forgot that five children were watching Playschool,
and made love, like teenagers, in the en suite, their
true function defined at last. Then, they were all
suddenly gone. I failed to face the day as I should —
oh, what strength visits us as we free ourselves
up for death.

That is suddenly me. Decided. Cooking casseroles,
needing to smell my babies one last time, to touch
scalp through sunbleached hair with my aging hands,
those hands that have touched too much, too often,
and yet not enough. Hours later, I will die, but for now,
life has found its true crevice, it assumes the shape of a
tharunka. Who would have thought that the most beautiful
sound in the world is that of the remote double garage
door: they are home.

In arcadia ego.

Another important moment has passed

I

The first time she wore a black velvet dress, and purple
shoes, and was married in Wandsworth Registry
one dark and snowy morning, like a peasant on
acid, drunk with gratitude yet full of spastic plots

for revenge on men who were already dead. What
was this madness? The groom spent his wedding
night singing in his car beneath Putney Bridge,
his bride asleep in a bathtub, empty bottles of

champagne and full packets of condoms her cackling
lovers, her happiness at having so successfully
changed her name quivering in her gut like a
virgin school girl about to kiss her cousin

for the very first time. Come dawn, besides them,
beyond their kitchen window, lay the forceful
Thames, working its python magic on their hearts:
Forget everything but Agincourt, let us reproduce.

II

In the kingdom of animals, she tried to find proof
of friendship. Once, she saw a tigress asleep at
the zoo, with six piglets dressed in fake tiger
coats on her belly. This must be how it is done,

she decided, and prayed for new skin. But then she
remembered her dog and his inability to hate sheep
and what this meant in terms of status. On a farm,
it is better to never spoil the dog with play and easier

to believe in the Spartan authority of outside toilets
than it is to endorse love. Lessons are learnt, planes
are caught, men are fucked, new horizons sucked dry
and marriages made. Her friends had chosen to defer

Gallipoli and Munich and raced to her wedding, bartering
with a storm-choked Channel that tried to throw them
back upon themselves, but they made it, they cast wishes:
It does not do, to dishonour hope, to unfasten celebration.

III

It came to pass that decades later she found the
remembrance of the webbed tragedies of pregnancies
and postnatal depressions and the sloppy suiciding
of her veteran friends just plain taxing. Marrying

for a second time in a bridal gown on Wategos Beach
the same man who still liked to sing under bridges
and kissed her oval breasts immer noch despite the knives
of life seemed like sense made regency, decision made. She

bequeathed the black velvet heirloom to her eldest
granddaughter *I have mended it for you darling* and
kissed her husband's salty lips. They grow macadamias
now on fields where cows once coupled, where they

had formerly harvested magic mushrooms. All this is not
forgotten but Richmond Clinic is full of drugged dreamers
from enslaved communes that had forsaken salvation:
And the dress sang, Oh bless me, for I will sin again.

petition

to remind ourselves that we need things, and that this need is born of a sense of our own insufficiency, to remind ourselves that to lay our hopes and dreams and desires before god is to know their true character, is to question the very desiring of them, to remind ourselves that when we wish, we must be willing to receive, as if our hearts were holy jelly and we knew what we should truly set them on . . .

The rowers are girls

Entrails of a meal,
all done, your small
teenage hands pick at
remains of zucchini,
now amoeba shaped, while
you blabber your blubber
about which high school
matters. To you, choice
is supermarket simple.
To me, alone in this decision,
your fathers elsewhere, it
is a peat bog of horror. It is
Friday nights and Southern
Comfort and Coke and will-
you-suck-my-cock terrorism,
teachers only remotely down
from the commune with their
yoghurt sensibilities, or fresh
like hard fruit from their city
universities, The Saints our
only soundtrack, we were, are,
all stranded: but not these shiny
girls, the ones that shape your
chase, with their crisp uniforms,
their sunblessed boaters, the Air
Cadets, the Yarra River their
backyard. Did I mention
the Air Cadets? Your absent
fathers and their skill in
renouncing satellite
communications? Jesus only

knows where they both
are. Somewhere in Europe,
dancing to songs my
boyfriends once wrote,
after we'd been down the river.

May it bless you, baby, may it never flood: I had a river
by my high school as well. It liked to drown
cows. May Melbourne Girls School save you from
abortionists, from men who leave, may it fill your bank
accounts greensomely, commune you, and fire your
endorphins forever. For every boy you kiss from now until
the day you die will have been selected by this decision, to
renounce local, to hunt down the other. 'We all lived
like that in the past, and followed the impulses and
imaginations of our evil nature', Paul almost certainly
wrote, though some say it was Timothy. I once kissed
Timothy Pomeroy in the Grenfell Olympic Pool. I was
nine, oh, the resilient responsibilities of the Christian. I
once believed, was told by *Rolling Stone*, that twenty-four
hours after midnight, there will be a rose.

Rise on sunshine, row away. Until it has smelt you, this
    century has not yet blossomed.

My daughter the crack whore

When I was in primary school I learnt how to make perfume
from the chemist's daughter, Christine. Flour and water and
rose petals crushed together in old empty jars from the
pharmacy. There was a magic ingredient she would never
reveal because I could run faster than her.

Later, in high school, I knew another Christine, my best friend,
who also didn't really like me that much, but still bothered me
with her razor and her holy secrets. Better science than perfume
was all the boys who chased me and my Christines: kissing when
caught was compulsory, was the true sport.

This is where all girls learn to hate men, at recess, after
Vegemite sandwiches, and before menstruation learnt how
to spoil the beauty of white underwear. This is where girls
learn the slant of horizontal hostility, behind the bike shed,
where everyone smells of smoke and venom.

Another planet: at school today my daughter was chased by a
dashing boy. He caught her. She would not kiss. *Your parents
are rapists and you are a little bitch. Piss off you crack whore.*
It was the first time she ever sobbed, dobbed. The headmistress
said *Be nice to him please. He doesn't have a mother.*

I will call that woman Christine from now on.

Advice for Mondays

Shark bait. There she was, waiting to die,
knitting with the patience of a woman who
has forgotten her marsh of unfinished business,
thinking up a list of suburban victory. Click. Clack.

> Buy wine
> Get photos
> Write thank yous
> Phone bank
> Etcetera, ce sera, sera

All of a sudden, a long lost apology came knock knock
knocking at the door, but she pushed the wrong button
and instead, it said:

> Please sir
> May I have some more
> Please
> More please?

Slam city slut put on some lipstick and went
to Ballina Fair, had it printed on a T-shirt, then
had sex with someone who wasn't her husband,
in the disabled toilet. More, please.

Give it back

She didn't believe me,
that I knew it was
off the map, my pain,
on its way to galaxies
where foreign plants
are cultivated, where
their fronds can kill.
In fact, I had one inside
me, I think. Yes. I
had been there and
back, under anaesthetic,
and now I was
inhabited by an alien
cousin of aloe vera,
turned bad, its
flesh responsible for
my black jelly
grape rock of pain.
I fainted, in Coles,
dead flat with it,
next to the compost
in aisle nine, smelling
of smart fear. She
changed her mind,
triffid woman, after
that story, too late,
though, for the antibiotics
to harvest their healthiest
crop, to stop simple from
turning stupendous.
I was infected with

something far greater
than need for your giant
drugs, than 'post-
operative' this and
'it's not my fault' that,
and its name was
sorrow. Of all my hurts—
where do they bury
your womb, anyway,
what rites do they
observe?—this one
was smartest.

The gods know who began this quarrel

Speculating endpoints, the woman involved, tentatively,
with her cold coffee, suddenly remembers her own heartbeat

as she spies upon the woman opposite her. She tries her
newspaper again, but does not really understand money

markets or tourism and the woman she can't stop sneaking
looks at has started softly crying. Her baby is dying, in

the hospital around the corner, it is not her fault, she has
been sent out of paediatric intensive care while they

perform some final, hopeless, intrusive tests. Testing
theories, hunting life, the crying woman writes in a small

book with a colourful silken cover. She writes with a blunt
pencil, she will not stop, she knows she is being spied

upon by a stranger who is ignoring her coffee, a stranger
who is tapping her feet like mad women do, as though

there is sex involved, and unconsumed tablets in her
handbag. The handbag is red, everything will be read.

Take this, write this, in remembrance of me.

As thin and fragile as wet newspaper, she waited for her mother, one day soon after man had walked on the moon

My mother said she was sorry, she regretted her 1970s
parenting full of Benson & Hedges and diets that involved
only biscuits and strange men in the bathroom. Mother mine,

insect with crisp red wings and black dots, how many wishes
did I waste on you? The first time, it felt like evolution, as I
stood at the school gates shedding history, *where are you*

where are you where are you, tight long socks, too big
uniform, resentful pigtails, dancing freckles, hand-me-down
brown samsonsite schoolcase, with no food in it. The sun

was kicking mountains away—would you come before
proper dark? I needed to pee, but would not run to the
toilets, my vigilance rewarded with hot trickles leaking

through the tight promise of white cottontail panties. I have
two legs and you have six. *Ladybird ladybird fly away home,*
Your children are waiting and your husband is gone. Years later,

I would marry a German and my tongue would learn his polka—
marienkäfer sounds better than ladybug—but *you bug me lady*
he said one day, and left. Better than never to have come.

Six brittle legs you have, none of them walking my way to collect
me. The sky lost its blue. Away you flew. As the first star cursed,
there you came, BKS818, too late.

Silence as sepia

He said (he was on his fifth drink) as the
galahs kamikazied the fruit trees, that goods
are not distributed evenly among the dead. At

first, it was just ancestors who were honoured
with origamied statues of apology, but Chairman
Mao put a stop to that singularity: let us not forget

our saviour warriors. No matter, we have
always prayed in pools of blood. Funerals do
that to you, make you wet with regret, with

life, for life. Why stop at five when you
can fathom the benefits of ten more? Drink
up, drink me up, Uncle, ember me with your

desire. Touch me like you once touched your
wife, when she was the one you dodged the
draft for—what had you ever done before

you knew each other like you did with fistfuls
of stars on that tricky riverbank? It is harvest
time again. There was, is, always the rice to

worry about. Go home now, I plead. Pay some
respect to the muck that is all history, I prayed:
then you put your hand up my skirt. I could feel the

soft dirt on your fingers, twenty minutes before you
had thrown great clumps of it on the only witness
to us, your brother, my father. Your life has

leaked into mine and left its blueberry stain, so
what ancestral hope remains? Until I learn to wrest
fault from the stars, I only have you to blame.

Lycanthropic lazy Sunday, unseized

The quicksand of figurative expressions
(is your dog black or blue?) and the luck
or otherwise of omens (does your bitch
walk with pups?) ranges whole valleys of
virile beliefs, but presents no authoritative
                                    account of us.

To Horace now: he may have been born
free, but how much can one really love
Rome in such circumstances? The smell
of slave, how long is its gladiatorial grip?
Run Horace, run, leave your shield in
                                    the field.

If it is true that our grasp of what it is like
to undergo phenomenal states is supplied
to us through introspection, then let me
sleep besides your qualia before you go
home to her, to them. Let me assume the
                                    shape of a wolf.

On transgressions fatal to spiritual progress: a dramatic poem to read on Tuesdays

This is the story of Mary. Mary
loves to love. Mary loves men,
and sex, and babies. Mary loves.
This is her story, about how it
ended, one Monday in April,
that cruel bitch of a month.

DOCTOR	On a scale of one to ten?
PATIENT	It hurts too much too count.
DOCTOR	You're being difficult.
PATIENT	You're not helping me.
DOCTOR	It's quite normal for you to feel like this after major surgery.
PATIENT	That's not what you told me before. You said
DOCTOR	That you'll feel like a new woman. You will. Be patient.
PATIENT	It's been four weeks now.
DOCTOR	I don't think another round of codeine is going to help.
PATIENT	I fainted this morning. In Woolworths. In the frozen pea cabinet.

Pause

PATIENT	I don't want codeine I want you to tell me what's wrong with me.

Pause

PATIENT	My daughter thought I was dead.

DOCTOR	I need to examine you. Are you up to it? An internal examination?
PATIENT	I am such a glutton for it.
DOCTOR	OK. You know the drill.

Patient throws her clothes on the floor. Lies down.

PATIENT	Ready. Why aren't you ever sick? I hate you.
DOCTOR	I am. Sometimes. Here?

Patient groans

DOCTOR	How about here?

Patient groans

DOCTOR	And here?
PATIENT	Yes, lord, there.
DOCTOR	Out of ten?
PATIENT	Worse than childbirth.
DOCTOR	Does it hurt more when I press down

Patient groans an eight out of ten groan

DOCTOR	or after I release?

Patient groans a twelve out of ten groan

PATIENT	After. Jesus.
DOCTOR	OK. Get dressed. I'll help you down.

Patient defers. Doctor writes up notes.

PATIENT   It's an alien isn't it?
DOCTOR   No, it's not an alien.
PATIENT   A baby? Ectopic?
DOCTOR   It's a post-operative infection.
PATIENT   Maybe some of the frozen peas have
             found a better cavity to. To.

Doctor sighs

DOCTOR   It is not an alien or an ectopic pregnancy
             Mary. You've just had a hysterectomy. You
             can't have any more children. Mary?

Silence

PATIENT   I want to go home please.

Curtain

And that is the story of Mary. These days,
Mary loves to read feminist theory from
the early 1980s about what keeps women
oppressed and how addiction to love and
male approbation have an awful lot to
answer for. Mary still loves men, but they
don't love her. She has a wasteland where
her womb once was, and children away at
university, and she can't find her husband
what use sperm anyhow and all this does not

[72]

make for very good company. Crime, she likes to read about crime, too. The end.

intercession

to remind ourselves that the world has its needs, to remember that to recall before god the ills and distresses of the world will bring comfort and peace of mind, in between the bullets, to know that to listen is the most important part of prayer, and that if we let god into our waiting silence then . . .

As far as I can tell there is nothing wrong with me: fugue for dying soldiers to sing out loud, as well as being a cento, for Charlie

I

Welcome to a new kind of tension well maybe another point in a redneck agenda sing along to the ancient paranoia everything isn't meant to be OK don't want to be an American idiot this is going out to idiot America a new kind of nation dreams of tomorrow we're not the ones you're meant to follow we are the kids of war and peace as far I can tell but don't believe in me I don't feel any shame I won't apologise give me mary jane to keep me insane doing someone else's cocaine this is how I'm meant to be there is a parking lot at the centre of the earth everyone's heart doesn't beat the same I don't care if you don't I don't care if you don't I don't care if you don't I don't care if you don't care I don't care I care I care where is the jesus of suburbia the space that is between insane and insecure. I walk alone. It's only me, and I walk alone where have all the riots gone it's not over till you're underground this city's burning there is nothing left to analyze when September ends wake me up jesus, suburbia I made a point to burn all of the photographs *One two three four.*

I took you shopping for maps in Covent Garden of the secret war zones but I ask you, boyfriend, what good is a *New York Times* corporate Amex when the enemy's cock is in your mouth?

II

This is our lives in paradise and you thought you were on holiday at the end of another lost highway no one really seems to care hypocrite we are the kids of war and peace dearly beloved are you listening am I retarded or am I just overjoyed one two three four but not this time I beg to dream and differ I don't feel any shame I won't apologize when you've been victimized death from another *you're leaving you're leaving you're leaving* heart I read the words on the bathroom wall holy scriptures of the shopping mall if you don't I don't care if you don't I don't care if you don't I don't care can I get another amen *amen* boulevard of broken dreams the only one that walks besides me my shadow sometimes I wish that someone up there will find me. To die without a name. Nobody likes you. She's an extraordinary girl she's all alone again some days she feels like dying she gets so sick of crying letterbomb letterbomb everyone left you they're all out without you having fun *Uh huh Uh huh.*

Your wife is pregnant, boyfriend, and here you are off on your boys' own adventure Gulf War Mark II how much did they pay you for the book contract and is it worth it?

III

City of the dead signs leading to nowhere the centre of the earth is the end of the world out of homes from the middle east and I don't believe I don't care I don't care and that's my best excuse to live and not to not to not to die in tragedy to run away to fight what you believe and I and I and I lost I lost your eyes your eyes a million hours of guitars there's a flag wrapped around a score of men to live and die without a name we are the kids of war and peace not this time believe if you don't I don't care if you don't I don't care if you don't I don't care *Zieg Heil* to the president gasman the reverend from

California has the floor hey hey hey this is the dawning of the rest of our lives from the hollow lies I beg to dream and differ *kill all the fags who disagree* I walk alone another protester has crossed the line I wrote the holy scriptures of the shopping mall when the city sleeps make believe as far as I can tell there is nothing wrong with me this is how I am supposed to be this dirty town is burning down in my years recital establishment cigarettes I am a son of a bitch and Edgar Allan Poe I'll give you something to cry about give me Novocaine take the pressure from the swelling tell me that I won't feel a thing the sensation's overwhelming everything will be all right she's the symbol of resistance and she's hanging on my eye like a hand grenade falling from the stars here comes the rain again please call me only if you are coming home you taught me how to live in the streets of shame where you lost your dreams in the rain rock and roll remember whatever it seems like forever no regrets *clap clap clap bang bang bang*

It's kind of all over now, boyfriend, Detroit is your war zone once again, arrogance is an evolutionary asset I grant but what do you tell your daughter, what will you tell your godson, about the shape and taste of absence, and the stories you once told? Or do you tell them to listen to Green Day? Behold.

PS Who am I to criticize you for whoring your way to Babylon?

Love Fuck Theory

Gone.
Fuck
you
I
say
drink
all
day
piss
your
life
away
stay
unhappy
forget
you're
with
me
read
my
smart
books
kiss
me
back
with
stale
theory
query
me
query

you
query
every
fucking
thing
make
me
late
for
my
lectures
yeah
make
me
hum
good
one
but
that
night
cost
four
hundred
and
fifty
pounds
who
wouldn't
come?

Now
I
do
your
washing,
you're
home
with
your
wife
in
a
metropolis
where
the
women
are
smart
and
the
talk
is
forever
cheap
so
can
you
convince
me
that
all

the
truths
that
beguiled
our
world
with
that
greatest
of
heroins
'Hope'
have
not
limped
back
to
the
loser's
shed
defeated
'nil all'
for
eternity?

Maybe. But you stroked me to sleep and wrote an entire book
on my back, it entered my blood (knowledge becomes me),
I glow I deliver I quiver with the memory of you as I talk
theory to babies. Listen. Up. They are (fuck) the future and I
am their trust, drowned in you. Now, I ain't no feminist fuck
theory kiss me better monograph me let me write my lies do

your own fucking washing. Too late. I have already sucked your collars clean, leeching memory from inanimacy while you talk divorce in the city of dark tides. And me (southern desire)? I wipe my baby girl's bum and whisper to her (ssshhhh)

love
love
love
love

(the promise of)

return.

Do not waste this, your second chance

Dingoes on the beach: this is not what we came here for
But you drive in that Stradbroke direction, to collect her
Beware the new roads, drive safe, do not forget the law
And I will forgive your slap, if you love her back, my daughter.

But you drive in that Stradbroke direction, to collect her
Sea snake you, highly poisonous — water is sometimes dew
And I will forgive your slap, if you love her back, my daughter
3000 snake bites a year in this country; none of them find you.

Sea snake you, highly poisonous—water is sometimes dew
Remember those redback spider bites? Corrugated iron hope
3000 snake bites a year in this country; none of them find you
Mop us up, before the away side wins, before we discover rope.

Remember those redback spider bites? Corrugated iron hope
Are you there yet? Kiss her. Tell her she is loved. Pretty promise
Mop us up, before the away side wins, before we discover rope
What use are legs when we float in jam? Quicksand tides, bliss.

To survive all those drunken years better, why not just kill him?
Beware the new roads, drive safe, do not forget the law
The police will always be there, so hold love, its shiny pin—
Dingoes on the beach: this is not what we came here for.

In the human way

You grumbled tartan nonsense
while I replastered and prayed, but
how does one choose a coffin for a baby?
I went to the funeral, it was in Tintenbar
Hall, it still smelt of a twenty-first birthday
bash from the 1970s, stale beer amongst
the tears. They have another
baby, now, I know, but on
that day as they talked
and offered their grief around
I burrowed into the daffodil glory of their
transubstantive offerings, their memories
the only loaf left in their life. On that
day, while you mowed the lawn,
I wept and prayed, and asked
God to bless them with the will
to stay married, to let them not
cry themselves dead for forty days and
forty nights. As the reluctant
mourners turned for home the gravel
hissed betrayal in the carpark and
I wondered what colour you
had painted the nursery—was it
scarlet, the colour of our trespass?—
and hoped that your labours worked,
like an egg on French toast, to
disguise the true ingredients of
your own gone north, gone south,
gone east, gone goodly west loss.
They sleep a thousand miles away,
those other children of yours that

have been orphaned by adult
greed and our nonsense needs.
And all the while, you husband
this bush, this wild land, like no other,
with your own special hush.

Someone else's cool
for Amy

If you take this job, one day you'll be standing on the corner
of Plenty Road waiting for the 86 tram at an intersection to
kill all intersections, and you'll spy, waiting for the lights, first
in line, a plumber, 'Joe the Plumber', in his fluorescent green
ute, and sitting placidly next to him, moronic with boredom,
is his sad daughter. She has end-of-the-day pigtails and a
grubby-collared high school uniform and, really, could do
with some braces, bless her. *Why don't you just move to Byron Bay
and be done with it?* you will think, *If I was a plumber that's what
I'd do. Fix shit and surf.* You will think this, you stupid woman,
you who can't even afford a car (how do the students afford all
that petrol?) hence the tram, and the wait, and you standing
there thinking this despite the fact that you know, you
know, that all the teenagers in Byron Bay wish they were in
Sydney (note: not Melbourne) or New York, anywhere but this
suburban dustball on a late sunsplit afternoon. The pollution.
The pollution. Yarra Trams route 86 to Waterfront City
Docklands, stop #60, La Trobe University. You will stand there,
listening to Primal Scream on your pink ipod remembering
seeing them last time, in Brighton, across the road from
the Channel, suicidal grey, and forgetting that you decided
to write a book about a deranged Gillespie groupie and the
worship of all things primordial, all the time praying that this
green-uted life will not be your daughter's. That she will be
saved such intersections. You will stand there twisting in the
heat and choking on everybody's urgent exiting, suddenly
knowing that leaving Stoke Newington Church Street and
St Mary's Church of England infants school where she was
the only white girl in her class was the dumbest-arsed thing
you ever did. To never again sit across from the school in Café
Vortex, chowing down to an egg and bacon sandwich with

the hum of your girlfriends also fresh from the school run, their sweet talk like birdsong in a cut-glass vase, in between breastfeeding and smiling at the singer from Cornershop who is smoking and drinking coffee and writing lyrics in Punjabi, and laughing with his mate, to never again be so close to your own shimmer, your true quickening, is irredeemable sin. Or, it would be. If you take this job, that is. But, there is this, also, to consider, that she may never know the lonely lusting for honeyed Hackney evenings and the quicksand pull of long summers in fifty-foot gardens full of French wine and London's naughty truck with itself, your daughter, she may never credit it: all such loss is someone else's cool. She may after all prefer Berlin. For such foolish things, I pray.

Why so close to all this traffic?

The burning

The fruit trees in Tante's city garden were harbingers of
schnapps, and the 'knopf-in-ohr' inheritances were
just teddies, simply there, long loved, bald with it
and eager for the possibilities that other owners might
reincarnate within them, the chance of redemption.

The harpsichord partly hid the painting of the two brothers,
two sisters, and the joyous capture of Aryan innocence,
shining brightly in the famous gold town, full of
the graves, now, of Jewish jewellers, withering wealth,
abundant art, civilised cemeteries. Lemon juiced youth.

The cross in the cemetery is an alien angel of the south,
seventeen feet high, at its feet the story speaks, one soaring
foot for every thousand dead, ten minutes of Bomber Harris's
revenge for Coventry, perfected menace returned in walls
of pretty fire, furnacing the endless pop of hopeful daffodils.

The girl, my daughter, belongs to them — the painting, the
people, the dead, the living, the daffodils, the blue-grassed
graves of her ancestors — she longs for them, for their
promise of 'friede, freude, eierkuchen', and the mirth of
anything that is not an ocean, pacific and lacking in debt.

The black forest has a blood that is also hers. I pray through
its crow coloured paths for a prouder recall, of genetic music
and century-deep intellects that may menace yet also fund her
soul. Your poetry is your own, my child, but tread softly to all
those Russian fronts, lest the bones you snap be your very own.

The leavetaking: a fairytale

Those boots. Imagine this:
If she hadn't betrayed
you and love had instead
done its gold-panning
prosperous thing, you
would still be there in the
halo of Edinburgh, your
life, full, beery, and bright
with autodidactic glory and
the wit of nursing your children
away from harm. Further.

Those hands. It has come to this:
There you are, in the tropical
cardboard of Brisbane International,
another head with its endless
sob of farewell upon your chest,
concrete with grief, losing them,
again, forever and ever gone.
Father. And this is just what
you will do: Let them. Go.
Those boots, they were
made for walking.

This is not a la mama play

If she were ever to publish a postcard
advertising her wares, what picture
would she choose, which text? 'Mary Jane
is an artist and writer whose work
utilises emerging and traditional technologies
and' and what? That looking at her dressed up
in her performance poetess petticoat
will make you think of nothing but sex?
It is true though: buying a book of her poems
will feel like you've been eligible for and paid off
a mortgage. It will feel better than an
affair of the heart. It is sure to be corporeal.

Real is now for Mary Jane, alas. Although married to
an artist of sorts (well, he teaches) a handsome, talented,
lost man, she is no poet and owns no lingerie of note but
nevertheless is instinctual enough to know that the man
sitting opposite her in her kitchen, at her table, does
not deserve his wealth. He leans forward
to pass her his removals quote and his aftershave
nearly kills her. She wonders if she could manage to
suck his cock, and if this would be worth three
thousand dollars to him. No. It would have to
be sex. Endless anal sex, surely, for three thousand. God.

Moving sucks.

Your mileage may vary

It's ten in the morning, spring is yawning, but
August has its Antarctic southern pull and this
is how I suddenly recollect you, girlfriend, jogging
in Hyde Park through six a.m. snowfalls with
a yellow waterproof walkman. Melbourne,
in this other century, has coffee that reanimates
life, but I remember us, then, when London did
not do lattes, in squalid South Kensington
bedsits, full of tampons and surfboards and
stray Australians. Like us. I see you getting ready
for Friday night, super secretary on the loose,
watch out Britain, we plan to rape all your
drunken soldiers. One day you just said 'America',
packed your weaponry, and left. I still have your
letters with their capacious descriptions of hospital
walls and interplanetary drugs and the interior
styling ambitions of airport bathrooms, and wonder
if this is why you did not invite me, your only true
bridesmaid, to your wedding. I hope he is kind to you,
this victor, that he holds your hand beyond childbirth,
that he is worth every plane I ever missed because
of your high heels, and our now dismissed high hells.

What blood knows

Good friends, my ship is on fire,
but the language of sorrow is a
moist, useless thing. Except when

you speak—*you do not trust me,
mother*—and truth becomes life's
largest task. You scream and cry

and swear, and one day soon your
eleven-year-old mouth will not fear
soap, will never cease to speak. A

late assignment on Victorian Tourism?
It's my fault, you hate me, I forgot to
buy coloured cardboard, everything

is somehow impossible. I am to blame,
I did that to you, to your world. Faith is
conviction enough to part all seas, but I

will never love your father again. Promises
promises. So I sleepwalked you to another
land, it is full of brown snakes and black

snakes and beaches named inventively
after mileage. This is your daily bread,
so do your homework, my darling, write

of those crumbling apostles circled by
great white sharks, lose your language,
kill all uprisings of love for me. But

do this—*sleep on your left side, keep your sword hand free*. This is only episode nine of 'Blood as Smoke'.

Good decisions also get you stuck in traffic

Will you come, with me, can I buy you
a drink? Last class, and all, a thank you,
he says. He has some days worth of Hollywood
beard on his face. Would you like to come
to the bar with me? Would you? I would like
that, I say. But I can't, I'm terribly sorry.
Thank you anyway, *darling*, I almost say. Why
not? Please? Come on. Why not? Because you are
my student. Because I am married. Because
I have to pick the children up. Because because.
Because I don't have a womb anymore, because
it is not the 1970s, and besides, when you
were starting high school I had finished
my PhD. Fuck off with your pleases.

I do not tell him that if he asks me, three times,
I will say yes. If he asks me while the galahs
are screeching and he has sought me out,
deliberately, more than twice, and that if he
keeps looking at me like that, then on the third
ask, I will acquiesce. I do not tell him that I already
know what will happen, that I will begin to be
happy and spend longer each day forgetting
small baby coffins, and the clods of earth that
shit upon them. I do not tell him that it will be
so good, I know, that the moon will choose
a new colour, a higher metal, with which to line
itself, because of us, and what will pass, and
what happens to silver. I say nothing.

I stand there, and say nothing. He hands me a
note. I give it back. I say, write to your parents,
write a story instead. Tell everything. It is what
I have been saying all semester. It is all I have ever
said. He strokes my wrist, I change my mind. I
take the note back, I put it in my pocket. Nick
Cave writes songs about women like me, I
say, loose, lousy women who squander
themselves looking for love, who feast on it
away from home, returning to their husbands
with secret smiles sneaking up the sides of
their shiny, sly mouths. Who wants to be a
character in someone else's song? That will be
me, tomorrow, I think.

His mates come up. They ask for extensions on
their essays. Piss off, he says. Fill in the forms, I say.
I forget everything, anything you ever say to me, unless
you write it down. We all know that it is only the reading
that matters. That, and that you should not flirt with
love when you can not even afford a hotel room. But
what good is money and rooms when all you do
with them is fuck your way through the rape of Paris,
like Sartre and de Beauvoir? I am a good girl, a brain
and blowjob girl, I have never been into Simone and her
sluttery. Plus, I will not ever write about what I know we
will do. I don't even have a pen. But then, there, on the bitumen
of the car park, amongst the shattered gum leaves, lies a broken
biro. Runover, cracked. Only a bitch would ignore this.

Some things are beyond song's salvation.

CPSIA information can be obtained at www.ICGtesting.com
Printed in the USA
LVOW110529280112

266000LV00005B/5/P